THE 30-MINUTE SHAKESPEARE
THE TWO GENTLEMEN OF VERONA

"Nick Newlin's work as a teaching artist for Folger Education during the past thirteen years has provided students, regardless of their experience with Shakespeare or being on stage, a unique opportunity to tread the boards at the Folger Theatre. Working with students to edit Shakespeare's plays for performance at the annual Folger Shakespeare Festivals has enabled students to gain new insights into the Bard's plays, build their skills of comprehension and critical reading, and just plain have fun working collaboratively with their peers.

Folger Education promotes performance-based teaching of Shakespeare's plays, providing students with an interactive approach to Shakespeare's plays in which they participate in a close reading of the text through intellectual, physical, and vocal engagement. Newlin's *The 30-Minute Shakespeare* series is an invaluable resource for teachers of Shakespeare, and for all who are interested in performing the plays."

ROBERT YOUNG, PH.D.
DIRECTOR OF EDUCATION
FOLGER SHAKESPEARE LIBRARY

The Two Gentleman of Verona: The 30-Minute Shakespeare
ISBN 978-1-935550-25-9
Adaptation, essays, and notes ©2018 by Nick Newlin

Cover design by Sarah Juckniess
Printed in the United States of America

Distributed by Consortium Book Sales & Distribution
www.cbsd.com

NICOLO WHIMSEY PRESS
www.30MinuteShakespeare.com

Art Director: Sarah Juckniess
Managing Editors: Katherine Little, Leah Gordon

THE TWO GENTLEMEN of VERONA

THE 30-MINUTE SHAKESPEARE

Written by **WILLIAM SHAKESPEARE**

Abridged AND Edited
by **NICK NEWLIN**

Nicolo Whimsey
Press

Brandywine, MD

To the students,
faculty, and staff
at Benjamin Banneker
Academic High School
in Washington, D.C.

for bringing life
to Shakespeare

Special thanks to Joanne Flynn, Bill Newlin, Eliza Newlin Carney, William and Louisa Newlin, Michael Tolaydo, Hilary Kacser, Sarah Juckniess, Katherine Little, Eva Zimmerman, Leah Gordon, Julie Schaper and all of Consortium, Leo Bowman and the students, faculty, and staff at Banneker Academic High School, and Robert Young Ph.D., and the Folger Shakespeare Library, especially the wonderful Education Department.

✳ TABLE OF CONTENTS

✳ NO EXPERIENCE NECESSARY

I was not a big "actor type" in high school, so if you weren't either, or if the young people you work with are not, then this book is for you. Whether or not you work with "actor types," you can use this book to stage a lively and captivating thirty-minute version of a Shakespeare play. No experience is necessary.

When I was about eleven years old, my parents took me to see Shakespeare's *Two Gentlemen of Verona*, which was being performed as a Broadway musical. I didn't comprehend every word I heard, but I was enthralled with the language, the characters, and the story, and I understood enough of it to follow along. From then on, I associated Shakespeare with *fun*.

Of course Shakespeare is fun. The Elizabethan audiences knew it, which is one reason he was so popular. It didn't matter that some of the language eluded them. The characters were passionate and vibrant, and their conflicts were compelling. Young people study Shakespeare in high school, but more often than not they read his work like a text book and then get quizzed on academic elements of the play, such as plot, theme, and vocabulary. These are all very interesting, but not nearly as interesting as standing up and performing a scene! It is through performance that the play comes alive and all its "academic" elements are revealed. There is nothing more satisfying to a student or teacher than the feeling of "owning" a Shakespeare play, and that can only come from performing it.

But Shakespeare's plays are often two or more hours long, making the performance of an entire play almost out of the question. One can perform a single scene, which is certainly a good start, but what about the story? What about the changes a character goes through as the play progresses? When school groups perform one scene unedited, or when they lump several plays together, the audience can get lost. This is why I have always preferred to tell the story of the play.

The 30-Minute Shakespeare gives students and teachers a chance to get up on their feet and act out a Shakespeare play in half an hour, using his language. The emphasis is on key scenes, with narrative bridges between scenes to keep the audience caught up on the action. The stage directions are built into this script so that young actors do not have to stand in one place; they can move and tell the story with their actions as well as their words. And it can all be done in a classroom during class time!

That is where this book was born: not in a research library, a graduate school lecture, a professional stage, or even an after-school drama club. All of the play cuttings in *The 30-Minute Shakespeare* were first rehearsed in a D.C. public high school English class, and performed successfully at the Folger Shakespeare Library's annual Secondary School Shakespeare Festival. The players were not necessarily "actor types." For many of them, this was their first performance in a play.

Something almost miraculous happens when students perform Shakespeare. They "get" it. By occupying the characters and speaking the words out loud, students gain a level of understanding and appreciation that is unachievable by simply reading the text. That is the magic of a performance-based method of learning Shakespeare, and this book makes the formerly daunting task of staging a Shakespeare play possible for anybody.

With *The 30-Minute Shakespeare* book series I hope to help teachers and students produce a Shakespeare play in a short amount of time, thus jump-starting the process of discovering the beauty, magic, and fun of the Bard. Plot, theme, and language reveal themselves through the performance of these half-hour play cuttings, and everybody involved receives the priceless gift of "owning" a piece of Shakespeare. The result is an experience that is fun and engaging, and one that we can all carry with us as we play out our own lives on the stages of the world.

NICK NEWLIN
Brandywine, MD
March 2010

CHARACTERS IN THE PLAY

The following is a list of characters that appear in this cutting of The Two Gentlemen of Verona.

Nineteen actors performed in the original production. This number can be increased to about thirty or decreased to about thirteen by having actors share or double roles.

For the full breakdown of characters, see Sample Program.

JULIA: Beloved of Proteus; disguises herself as Sebastian

LUCETTA: Seamstress; waiting woman to Julia

LAUNCE: Clownish servant to Proteus, joined by his dog Crab

CRAB: Launce's dog

SPEED: Servant to Valentine

SILVIA: Daughter to the Duke of Milan; beloved of Valentine

VALENTINE: A gentleman of Verona who woos Silvia and is banished by the Duke

PROTEUS: A gentleman of Verona; in love with Julia, then Silvia

DUKE OF MILAN: Father to Silvia; banishes Valentine for wooing Silvia

MUSICIANS

NARRATOR

✳ **SCENE 1.** (ACT I, SCENE II)

Verona. Julia's garden.

STAGEHANDS *set table and two chairs center stage, placing flowers, tea pot, and cups atop table.*

Enter **NARRATOR** *from stage rear, coming downstage center.*

NARRATOR

>Our play begins in Julia's garden, where Julia receives a love letter from Proteus. Lucetta, Julia's woman-in-waiting deals with Julia's mixed feelings.

SOUND OPERATOR *plays* Sound Cue #1 ("Merry domestic music").

Exit **NARRATOR** *stage left.*

Enter **JULIA** *and* **LUCETTA** *from stage right.* **JULIA** *sits in chair stage left;* **LUCETTA** *sits in chair stage right.*

JULIA

>But say, Lucetta, now we are alone,
>Wouldst thou then counsel me to fall in love?

LUCETTA

>Ay, madam; so you stumble not unheedfully. *(dusts)*

JULIA

>Of all the fair resort of gentlemen
>That every day with parle encounter me,
>In thy opinion which is worthiest love?

LUCETTA

Please you repeat their names, I'll show my mind
According to my shallow simple skill.

JULIA

What think'st thou of the rich Mercatio?

LUCETTA

Well of his wealth; but of himself, so-so.

JULIA

What think'st thou of the gentle Proteus?

LUCETTA

Of many good I think him best.

JULIA

Why, he, of all the rest, hath never moved me.

LUCETTA

Yet he, of all the rest, I think, best loves ye.
            (mysteriously)
Peruse this paper, madam.

LUCETTA *gives* JULIA *a letter.*

JULIA

Say, say, who gave it thee?

JULIA *opens the letter and glances at it.*

LUCETTA

Sir Valentine's page; and sent, I think, from Proteus.
He would have given it you; but I, being in the way,
Did in your name receive it: pardon the fault, I pray.

JULIA

> Now, by my modesty, a goodly broker!
> Dare you presume to harbor wanton lines?
> To whisper and conspire against my youth?
> There, take the paper: see it be return'd;
> Or else return no more into my sight.

JULIA *gives the letter back to* LUCETTA.

> Will you be gone?

Exit LUCETTA *stage right, accidentally dropping the letter on her way out.*

JULIA

> And yet I would I had o'erlook'd the letter: *(paces,*
>   *picking up, then putting down, the letter)*
> Fie, fie, how wayward is this foolish love,
> That, like a testy babe, will scratch the nurse; *(sits)*
> How churlishly I chid Lucetta hence,
> When inward joy enforced my heart to smile!
> My penance is to call Lucetta back
> And ask remission for my folly past. *(stands; faces*
>   *stage right)*
> What ho! Lucetta!

Enter LUCETTA *from stage right, picking up the dropped letter.*

LUCETTA

> What would your ladyship?

JULIA

> Some love of yours hath writ to you in rhyme.
>   *(reaches for letter)*

LUCETTA

> That I might sing it, madam, to a tune.

LUCETTA *pulls the letter away teasingly.*

JULIA

Let's see your song.

LUCETTA *offers the letter, but pulls it away again.*

How now, minion!

JULIA *sits and turns her back to* LUCETTA.

LUCETTA

Keep tune there still, so you will sing it out:
And yet methinks I do not like this tune.

JULIA

You do not? *(stands; turns to confront* LUCETTA*)*

LUCETTA

No, madam; 'tis too sharp. *(stands; turns to* JULIA*)*

JULIA

You, minion, are too saucy. *(steps closer)*

LUCETTA *(steps closer; they are nose to nose)*

Nay, now you are too flat.

JULIA

This babble shall not henceforth trouble me:

JULIA *tears the letter into several pieces.*

Go get you gone, and let the papers lie:

Exit LUCETTA *stage right.*

O hateful hands, to tear such loving words!
I'll kiss each several paper for amends. *(kisses pieces
of letter)*
Look, here is writ—"kind Julia:"—unkind Julia!
And here is writ—"love-wounded Proteus:"—
Poor wounded name! My bosom, as a bed,
Shall lodge thee, till thy wound be throughly heal'd;
Lo, here in one line is his name twice writ,—
"Poor forlorn Proteus, passionate Proteus,
To the sweet Julia:"—that I'll tear away;—
And yet I will not, sith so prettily
He couples it to his complaining names.
Thus will I fold them one upon another:
(places pieces of letter together)
Now kiss, embrace, contend, do what you will.
(puts pieces of letter down)

Enter LUCETTA *from stage right.*

LUCETTA

What, shall these papers lie like tell-tales here?

JULIA

If you respect them, best to take them up.

LUCETTA

Nay, I was taken up for laying them down: *(pauses)*
Yet here they shall not lie, for catching cold.
(picks up the pieces)

JULIA

I see you have a month's mind to them.

LUCETTA

Ay, madam, you may say what sights you see;
I see things too, although you judge I wink.

JULIA

Come, come; will't please you go?

Exit JULIA *stage right;* LUCETTA *follows her.*

STAGEHANDS *remove table and chairs, then set bench center stage.*

✳ **SCENE 2.** (ACT II, SCENE III)

Verona. A street.

Enter **NARRATOR** *from stage rear, coming downstage center.*

NARRATOR

> Launce grieves that he must part with his family to travel with Proteus, his master. He chastises his dog, Crab, for not sharing his grief.

Exit **NARRATOR** *stage left.*

Enter **LAUNCE** *from stage rear, leading his dog. He ties* **CRAB** *to the bench and then sits next to him on the floor.*

LAUNCE

> I am going with Sir Proteus to the imperial's court. I think Crab my dog be the sourest-natured dog that lives: my mother weeping, my father wailing, our cat wringing her hands, yet did not this cruel-hearted cur shed one tear: he is a very pebble-stone, and has no more pity in him than a dog. Nay, I'll show you the manner of it. This shoe is my father. This shoe, with the hole in it, is my mother. I am the dog; no, the dog is himself, and I am the dog,—O, the dog is me, and I am myself. Now should I kiss my father; well, he weeps on. Now come I to my mother; well, I kiss her; why, there 'tis; here's my mother's breath up and down. Now the dog all this while sheds not a tear, nor speaks a word: but see how I lay the dust with my tears.

Enter SPEED *from stage rear.*

SPEED

Launce, away, away, aboard! Thy master is shipp'd, and thou art to post after with oars. What's the matter? Why weep'st thou, man? Away, ass! You'll lose the tide, if you tarry any longer.

LAUNCE

It is no matter if the tied were lost; for it is the unkindest tied that ever any man tied.

SPEED

What's the unkindest tide?

LAUNCE

Why, he that's tied here,—Crab, my dog.

SPEED

Tut, man, I mean thou'lt lose the flood: and, in losing the flood, lose thy voyage.

LAUNCE

Lose the tide, and the voyage, why, man, if the river were dry, I am able to fill it with my tears; if the wind were down, I could drive the boat with my sighs.

SPEED

Come, come away, man; I was sent to call thee.

LAUNCE

Sir, call me what thou darest. *(draws sword)*

SPEED

Wilt thou go?

LAUNCE *takes leash and starts to walk with* CRAB. *He falls down because the leash is still tied to the bench, but he gets back up and tries to regain his composure.*

LAUNCE
Well, I will go.

LAUNCE *unties* CRAB'S *leash and both exit stage left.*

STAGEHANDS *remove bench, then place throne center stage, with a chair on either side.*

✳ **SCENE 3.** (ACT II, SCENE IV)

Milan. The Duke's palace.

Enter NARRATOR *from stage rear, coming downstage center and leading* CRAB *on a leash.*

NARRATOR

Proteus arrives in Milan and is greeted by his best friend, Valentine, and Valentine's beloved, Silvia. Proteus immediately falls in love with Silvia.

Exit NARRATOR *and* CRAB *stage left.*

Enter SILVIA *and* VALENTINE *from stage rear.* SILVIA *sits in chair stage right and* VALENTINE *sits in chair stage left.*

SILVIA

Here comes the gentleman.

Enter PROTEUS *from stage right.* VALENTINE *goes to him, greeting him warmly.*

VALENTINE

Welcome, dear Proteus!
Mistress, I beseech you, entertain him
To be my fellow-servant to your ladyship.

SILVIA

Too low a mistress for so high a servant.

PROTEUS
> Not so, sweet lady; but too mean a servant
> *(kneels; kisses her hand)*
> To have a look of such a worthy mistress.

VALENTINE *(moves next to* **SILVIA***)*
> Leave off discourse of disability:
> Sweet lady, entertain him for your servant.

PROTEUS
> My duty will I boast of, nothing else.

SILVIA
> And duty never yet did want his meed:
> Servant, you are welcome to a worthless mistress.

SILVIA *gestures for* **PROTEUS** *to sit in stage right chair.*

PROTEUS
> I'll die on him that says so, but yourself.

SILVIA
> That you are welcome?

PROTEUS
> That you are worthless.

VALENTINE *coughs.*

SILVIA
> I'll leave you to confer of home affairs;
> When you have done, I look to hear from you.

PROTEUS
> We'll both attend upon your ladyship.

Exit SILVIA *stage right.*

VALENTINE *walks to Proteus's chair.*

VALENTINE
> Now, tell me, Proteus,
> How does your lady? And how thrives your love?

PROTEUS
> My tales of love were wont to weary you;
> I know you joy not in a love-discourse.

VALENTINE
> Ay, Proteus, but that life is alter'd now.
> > *(walks downstage center)*
> For, in revenge of my contempt of love,
> Love hath chased sleep from my enthralled eyes,
> And made them watchers of mine own heart's sorrow.
> O gentle Proteus, Love's a mighty lord,
> And hath so humbled me, as, I confess,
> Now can I break my fast, dine, sup, and sleep,
> Upon the very naked name of love.

PROTEUS *(walks to* VALENTINE*)*
> Enough; I read your fortune in your eye.
> Was this the idol that you worship so?
> > *(gestures to where* SILVIA *exited)*

VALENTINE
> Even she; and is she not a heavenly saint?

PROTEUS
> No; but she is an earthly paragon.

VALENTINE
> Call her divine.

PROTEUS

> I will not flatter her.

VALENTINE

> Then speak the truth by her: if not divine,
> Yet let her be a principality,
> Sovereign to all the creatures on the earth.

PROTEUS

> Except my mistress.
> Why, Valentine, what braggardism is this?

VALENTINE

> Pardon me, Proteus: all I can is nothing
> To her, whose worth makes other worthies nothing;
> She is alone.

PROTEUS

> Then let her alone.

VALENTINE

> Not for the world: why, man, she is mine own;
> And I as rich in having such a jewel
> As twenty seas, if all their sand were pearl,
> The water nectar, and the rocks pure gold.

PROTEUS

> But she loves you?

VALENTINE

> Ay, and we are betroth'd: nay, more, our marriage-hour,
> With all the cunning manner of our flight,
> Determined of; how I must climb her window,
> The ladder made of cords; and all the means
> Plotted and 'greed on for my happiness.

> Good Proteus, go with me to my chamber,
> In these affairs to aid me with thy counsel.

PROTEUS

> Go on before; I shall inquire you forth:
> And then I'll presently attend you.

VALENTINE

> Will you make haste?

PROTEUS

> I will.

Exit VALENTINE *stage right.*

> *(to audience)* Even as one heat another heat expels,
> Or as one nail by strength drives out another,
> So the remembrance of my former love
> Is by a newer object quite forgotten.
> Is it mine eye, or Valentine's praise,
> Her true perfection, or my false transgression,
> That makes me, reasonless, to reason thus?
> She's fair; and so is Julia, that I love,—
> That I did love, for now my love is thaw'd;
> Which, like a waxen image 'gainst a fire,
> Bears no impression of the thing it was.
> If I can check my erring love, I will;
> If not, to compass her I'll use my skill.

Exit PROTEUS *stage right.*

STAGEHANDS *remove throne.*

✳ SCENE 4. (ACT III, SCENE I)

Milan. An ante-room in the Duke's palace.

Enter NARRATOR *from stage rear, coming downstage center.*

NARRATOR
>Proteus betrays Valentine's elopement plans to
Silvia's father, the Duke of Milan, who banishes
Valentine. Proteus pretends to grieve with Valentine
and conveys him on his way to exile.

Exit NARRATOR *stage left.*

Enter DUKE OF MILAN *and* PROTEUS *from stage rear.* DUKE OF
MILAN *sits in chair stage left.*

DUKE OF MILAN
>Now, tell me, Proteus, what's your will with me?

PROTEUS *(bows; goes to his knees)*
>My gracious lord, that which I would discover
The law of friendship bids me to conceal.

PROTEUS *stands and moves closer to* DUKE OF MILAN *to tell him
a secret.*

>Know, worthy prince, Sir Valentine, my friend,
This night intends to steal away your daughter.

DUKE OF MILAN
>Proteus, I thank thee for thine honest care;

Upon mine honor, he shall never know
That I had any light from thee of this.

PROTEUS
Adieu, my lord; Sir Valentine is coming.

Exit PROTEUS *stage rear.*

Enter VALENTINE *from stage right, holding a letter.*

DUKE OF MILAN
Sir Valentine, whither away so fast?

VALENTINE *(bows swiftly and nervously)*
Please it your grace, there is a messenger
That stays to bear my letters to my friends,
And I am going to deliver them.

VALENTINE *starts to exit stage right.*

DUKE OF MILAN *(grabs the letter, stopping* VALENTINE*)*
What letter is this same? What's here?—"To Silvia"!
      (reads)
"My thoughts do harbor with my Silvia nightly;
My herald thoughts in thy pure bosom rest them;
I curse myself, for they are sent by me,
That they should harbor where their lord would be."
What's here?
"Silvia, this night I will enfranchise thee." *(angrily)*
Go, base intruder! Overweening slave!
      (rips letter and throws it to the ground)
If thou linger in my territories
By heaven, my wrath shall far exceed the love
I ever bore my daughter or thyself.
Be gone! I will not hear thy vain excuse;
But, as thou lovest thy life, make speed from hence.

Exit **DUKE OF MILAN** *stage rear.*

VALENTINE *(falls to his knees)*
> And why not death, rather than living torment?
> To die, is to be banish'd from myself;
> And Silvia is myself: banish'd from her,
> Is self from self: a deadly banishment!
> What light is light, if Silvia be not seen?
> What joy is joy, if Silvia be not by?
> Tarry I here, I but attend on death;
> But, fly I hence, I fly away from life.

Enter **PROTEUS** *and* **LAUNCE** *from stage right.*

PROTEUS
> Valentine!

VALENTINE
> No.

PROTEUS
> What then?

VALENTINE
> Nothing.

LAUNCE
> Can nothing speak? Master, shall I strike?
>> *(draws sword)*

PROTEUS
> Who wouldst thou strike?

LAUNCE *(looks around; points to* **VALENTINE***)*
> Nothing.

PROTEUS (*steps in front of* LAUNCE)
> Villain, forbear.
> Friend Valentine, a word.

VALENTINE
> My ears are stopp'd, and cannot hear good news,
> So much of bad already hath possess'd them.

LAUNCE (*confused*)
> Sir, there is a proclamation that you are vanish'd.

PROTEUS
> That thou art banished—O, that's the news!—
> From hence, from Silvia, and from me thy friend.

VALENTINE
> O, I have fed upon this woe already.

PROTEUS *kneels next to* VALENTINE *and places a hand on his shoulder.*

PROTEUS
> Cease to lament for that thou canst not help,
> Time is the nurse and breeder of all good.
> Here if thou stay, thou canst not see thy love;
> Besides, thy staying will abridge thy life.
> Hope is a lover's staff; walk hence with that.
> > (*helps* LAUNCE *to his feet*)
> Thy letters may be here, though thou art hence;
> Which, being writ to me, shall be deliver'd
> Even in the milk-white bosom of thy love.
> Come, Valentine.

VALENTINE
> O my dear Silvia! Hapless Valentine!

Exit VALENTINE *and* PROTEUS *stage left, with* PROTEUS *comforting* VALENTINE *as they go.*

LAUNCE *walks downstage center.*

LAUNCE *(to audience)*
> I am but a fool, look you; and yet I have the wit to
> think my master is a kind of knave.

Exit LAUNCE *stage left.*

STAGEHANDS *remove chairs, then set bench stage left in front of pillar.*

✳ **SCENE 5.** (ACT IV, SCENE II)

Milan. The court of the Duke's palace.

Enter **NARRATOR** *from stage rear, coming downstage center.*

NARRATOR
> Proteus and musicians serenade Silvia, as the Host and Julia, who is disguised as a male page, look on. The sight (and sounds) of Proteus's infidelity practically breaks poor Julia's heart.

Exit **NARRATOR** *stage left.*

Enter **PROTEUS** *and* **MUSICIANS** *from stage left, coming to center stage.*

PROTEUS *(to audience)*
> Already have I been false to Valentine,
> But Silvia is too fair, too true, too holy,
> To be corrupted with my worthless gifts.
> Now must we to her window,
> And give some evening music to her ear.
> *(to musicians)* Now, gentlemen,
> Let's tune, and to it lustily awhile.

The **MUSICIANS** *start to tune up quietly.*

Enter **HOST** *and* **JULIA**, *who is dressed in boy's clothes, from stage right.*

HOST

Now, my young guest, methinks you're allicholy: I
pray you, why is it?

JULIA

Marry, mine host, because I cannot be merry.

HOST

Come, we'll have you merry: I'll bring you where
you shall hear music, and see the gentleman that
you ask'd for.

JULIA

That will be music.

MUSICIANS *(singing while playing)*

Who is Silvia? What is she,
That all our swains commend her?
Holy, fair, and wise is she;
The heaven such grace did lend her,
That she might admired be.
Is she kind as she is fair?
For beauty lives with kindness.
Love doth to her eyes repair,
To help him of his blindness,
And, being help'd, inhabits there.
Then to Silvia let us sing,
That Silvia is excelling;
She excels each mortal thing
Upon the dull earth dwelling:
To her let us garlands bring.

MUSICIANS *exit stage rear, still playing their instruments.*

HOST

How now! Are you sadder than you were before?
How do you, man? The music likes you not.

JULIA.

You mistake; the musician likes me not.

HOST

Why, my pretty youth?

JULIA

He plays false, father.

HOST

How? Out of tune on the strings?

JULIA

Not so; but yet so false that he grieves my very
heart-strings.

HOST

You have a quick ear.

JULIA

Ay, I would I were deaf; it makes me have a slow
heart.

HOST and **JULIA** *stand behind stage right pillar, out of view of*
PROTEUS *and* **SILVIA**.

SILVIA *appears above, at her window.*

PROTEUS

Madam, good even to your ladyship.

SILVIA

Sir Proteus, as I take it.
What is your will?

PROTEUS

That I may compass yours.

SILVIA

You have your wish; my will is even this:
That presently you hie you home to bed.
Thou subtle, perjured, false, disloyal man!
Think'st thou I am so shallow, so conceitless,
To be seduced by thy flattery,
That hast deceived so many with thy vows?
Return, return, and make thy love amends.
I despise thee for thy wrongful suit.

PROTEUS

Madam, if your heart be so obdurate,
Vouchsafe me yet your picture for my love,
And to your shadow will I make true love.

JULIA *(to* HOST*)*

If 'twere a substance, you would, sure, deceive it,
And make it but a shadow, as I am.

SILVIA

I am very loath to be your idol, sir.

Exit SILVIA *stage left.* PROTEUS *pauses and then runs offstage after her.*

JULIA

Host, will you go?

HOST (*starts awake*)

> By my halidom, I was fast asleep.
> Trust me, I think 'tis almost day.

JULIA

> Not so; but it hath been the longest night
> That e'er I watch'd, and the most heaviest.

Exit JULIA *and* HOST *stage right.*

STAGEHANDS *move bench to center stage.*

✳ **SCENE 6.** (ACT V, SCENE IV)

The forest.

Enter NARRATOR *from stage rear, coming downstage center.*

SOUND OPERATOR *plays* Sound Cue #2 ("Mysterious forest music").

NARRATOR
> As Valentine watches from a hiding place,
> Proteus pleads for Silvia's love. Things get a little
> complicated, but don't worry, it's a Shakespearean
> comedy—human error is sure to result in
> forgiveness, not catastrophe!

Exit NARRATOR *stage left.*

Enter VALENTINE *from stage rear. He sits in front of stage right pillar.*

VALENTINE
> This shadowy desert, unfrequented woods:
> Here can I sit alone, unseen of any,
> And to the nightingale's complaining notes
> Tune my distresses and record my woes.
> Repair me with thy presence, Silvia!
> Thou gentle nymph, cherish thy forlorn swain!

A noise sounds from offstage left.

> Withdraw thee, Valentine: who's this comes here?

VALENTINE *hides behind stage right pillar.*

Enter PROTEUS, SILVIA, *and* JULIA, *still in boy's clothes, from stage left.* PROTEUS *and* SILVIA *sit on bench, while* JULIA *sits on the ground to their left.*

PROTEUS

Madam, vouchsafe me, for my meed, but one fair look.

VALENTINE *(aside)*

How like a dream is this I see and hear!

SILVIA

O miserable, unhappy that I am!

PROTEUS

Unhappy were you, madam, ere I came;
But by my coming I have made you happy.

SILVIA

By thy approach thou makest me most unhappy.

JULIA *(aside)*

And me, when he approacheth to your presence.

SILVIA *moves closer to the edge of bench, away from* PROTEUS.

SILVIA

Had I been seized by a hungry lion,
I would have been a breakfast to the beast,
Rather than have false Proteus rescue me.
O, Heaven be judge how I love Valentine,
Whose life's as tender to me as my soul;
I do detest false perjured Proteus!
Therefore be gone, solicit me no more.

PROTEUS

> O, 'tis the curse in love, and still approved,
> When women cannot love where they're beloved!

SILVIA

> When Proteus cannot love where he's beloved.
> Read over Julia's heart, thy first best love,
> Thou counterfeit to thy true friend!

PROTEUS

> In love
> Who respects friend?

SILVIA

> All men but Proteus.

PROTEUS

> Nay, if the gentle spirit of moving words
> Can no way change you to a milder form,
> I'll woo you like a soldier, at arms' end,
> And love you 'gainst the nature of love,—force thee
>   yield to my desire.

PROTEUS *lunges at* **SILVIA**, *who first eludes him and then attacks him.* **PROTEUS** *ends up on the ground with* **SILVIA** *stepping on him. He tries to escape her foot.*

SILVIA

> O heaven!

VALENTINE *(comes forward)*

> Ruffian, let go that rude uncivil touch,
> Thou friend of an ill fashion!

PROTEUS

> Valentine!

VALENTINE

> Thou common friend, that's without faith or love,
> Who should be trusted, when one's right hand
> Is perjured to the bosom?
> The private wound is deepest: O time most accurs'd!
> 'Mongst all foes that a friend should be the worst!

PROTEUS *(kneels in shame)*

> My shame and guilt confounds me.
> Forgive me, Valentine: if hearty sorrow
> Be a sufficient ransom for offense,
> I tender 't here; I do as truly suffer
> As e'er I did commit.

VALENTINE

> Then I am paid;
> And once again I do receive thee honest.
> Who by repentance is not satisfied
> Is nor of heaven nor earth, for these are pleased.
> By penitence th' Eternal wrath's appeased:
> And, that my love may appear plain and free,
> All that was mine in Silvia I give thee.

VALENTINE *takes* **SILVIA** *by the shoulders and presents her to* **PRO-**
TEUS, *still fearful after their earlier interaction.*

JULIA

> O me unhappy! *(faints)*

PROTEUS

> Look to the boy.

VALENTINE *(moves to* **JULIA***)*

> Why, boy! Why, wag! How now! What's the matter?
> Look up; speak.

JULIA

O good sir, my master charged me
To deliver a ring to Madam Silvia;
Which, out of my neglect, was never done.

PROTEUS

Where is that ring, boy?

JULIA

Here 'tis; this is it. *(gives ring to* **PROTEUS***)*

PROTEUS

How! Let me see:
Why, this is the ring I gave to Julia.

JULIA

O, cry you mercy, sir, I have mistook:
This is the ring you sent to Silvia. *(takes out a
          second ring)*

PROTEUS

But how camest thou by this ring? At my depart
I gave this unto Julia.

JULIA

And Julia herself did give it me;
And Julia herself hath brought it hither. *(removes hat)*

PROTEUS *(with recognition)*
How! Julia!

JULIA

Behold her that gave aim to all thy oaths,
And entertain'd 'em deeply in her heart:
How oft hast thou with perjury cleft the root!

O Proteus, let this habit make thee blush!
Be thou ashamed that I have took upon me
Such an immodest raiment, if shame live
In a disguise of love:
It is the lesser blot, modesty finds,
Women to change their shapes than men their minds.

PROTEUS

Than men their minds! 'Tis true. O heaven, were man
But constant, he were perfect! That one error
Fills him with faults; makes him run through all th' sins:
Inconstancy falls off ere it begins.
What is in Silvia's face, but I may spy
More fresh in Julia's with a constant eye?

VALENTINE

Come, come, a hand from either: *(joins their hands)*
Let me be bless'd to make this happy close;
'Twere pity two such friends should be long foes.

PROTEUS

Bear witness, Heaven, I have my wish for ever.

JULIA

And I mine.

Enter **DUKE OF MILAN** *from stage left, along with attendants.*
JULIA *hurriedly puts her hat back on.*

VALENTINE

It is my lord the duke.

DUKE OF MILAN

Sir Valentine!

VALENTINE

Come not within the measure of my wrath:
Do not name Silvia thine; if once again,
Verona shall not hold thee. Here she stands;
Take but possession of her with a touch:
I dare thee but to breathe upon my love.

DUKE OF MILAN

I do applaud thy spirit, Valentine,
And think thee worthy of an empress' love:
Know then, I here forget all former griefs,
Cancel all grudge, repeal thee home again.
Thou art a gentleman, and well derived;
Take thou thy Silvia, for thou hast deserved her.

VALENTINE

I thank your grace; the gift hath made me happy.
What think you of this page, my lord?

DUKE OF MILAN

I think the boy hath grace in him; he blushes.

VALENTINE

I warrant you, my lord, more grace than boy.

DUKE OF MILAN

What mean you by that saying?

JULIA *removes hat once more to reveal that she is a woman.*

VALENTINE

Please you, I'll tell you as we pass along,
That you will wonder what hath fortuned.
Come, Proteus; 'tis your penance but to hear
The story of your loves discovered:

That done, our day of marriage shall be yours;
One feast, one house, one mutual happiness.

MUSICIANS *(chanting)*
One peace, one house, one mutual happiness!

ALL *hold hands and bow. Exeunt.*

✳ PERFORMING SHAKESPEARE

BACKGROUND:
HOW *THE 30-MINUTE SHAKESPEARE* WAS BORN

In 1981 I performed a "Shakespeare Juggling" piece called "To Juggle or Not To Juggle" at the first Folger Library Secondary School Shakespeare Festival. The audience consisted of about 200 Washington, D.C. area high school students who had just performed thirty-minute versions of Shakespeare plays for each other and were jubilant over the experience. I was dressed in a jester's outfit, and my job was to entertain them. I juggled and jested and played with Shakespeare's words, notably Hamlet's "To be or not to be" soliloquy, to very enthusiastic response. I was struck by how much my "Shakespeare Juggling" resonated with a group who had just performed Shakespeare themselves. "Getting" Shakespeare is a heady feeling, especially for adolescents, and I am continually delighted at how much joy and satisfaction young people derive from performing Shakespeare. Simply reading and studying this great playwright does not even come close to inspiring the kind of enthusiasm that comes from performance.

Surprisingly, many of these students were not "actor types." A good percentage of the students performing Shakespeare that day were part of an English class which had rehearsed the plays during class time. Fifteen years later, when I first started directing plays in D.C. public schools as a Teaching Artist with the Folger Shakespeare Library, I entered a ninth grade English class as a guest and spent two or three days a week for two or three months preparing students for the Folger's annual Secondary School Shakespeare Festival. I have conducted this annual residency with the Folger ever since.

Every year for seven action-packed days, eight groups of students between grades seven and twelve tread the boards onstage at the Folger's Elizabethan Theatre, a grand recreation of a sixteenth-century venue with a three-tiered gallery, carved oak columns, and a sky-painted canopy.

As noted on the Folger website (www.folger.edu), "The festival is a celebration of the Bard, not a competition. Festival commentators—drawn from the professional theater and Shakespeare education communities—recognize exceptional performances, student directors, and good spirit amongst the students with selected awards at the end of each day. They are also available to share feedback with the students."

My annual Folger Teaching Artist engagement, directing a Shakespeare play in a public high school English class, is the most challenging and the most rewarding thing I do all year. I hope this book can bring you the same rewards.

GETTING STARTED: GAMES

How can you get an English class (or any other group of young people, or even adults) to start the seemingly daunting task of performing a Shakespeare play? You have already successfully completed the critical first step, which is buying this book. You hold in your hand a performance-ready, thirty-minute cutting of a Shakespeare play, with stage directions to get the actors moving about the stage purposefully. But it's a good idea to warm the group up with some theater games.

One good initial exercise is called "Positive/Negative Salutations." Students stand in two lines facing each other (four or five students in each line) and, reading from index cards, greet each other, first with a "Positive" salutation in Shakespeare's language (using actual phrases from the plays), followed by a "negative" greeting.

Additionally, short vocal exercises are an essential part of the preparation process. The following is a very simple and effective vocal warm-up: Beginning with the number two, have the whole group count to twenty using increments of two (i.e., "Two, four, six . . ."). Increase the volume slightly with each number, reaching top volume with "twenty," and then decrease the volume while counting back down, so that the students are practically whispering when they arrive again at "two." This exercise teaches dynamics and allows them to get loud as a group without any individual pressure. Frequently during a rehearsal period, if a student is mumbling inaudibly, I will refer back to this exercise as a reminder that we can and often do belt it out!

"Stomping Words" is a game that is very helpful at getting a handle on Shakespeare's rhythm. Choose a passage in iambic pentameter and have the group members walk around the room in a circle, stomping their feet on the second beat of each line:

Two **house**-holds, **both** a-**like** in **dig**-nity
In **fair** Ve-**ro**na **Where** we **lay** our **scene**

Do the same thing with a prose passage, and have the students discuss their experience with it, including points at which there is an extra beat, etc., and what, if anything, it might signify.

I end every vocal warm-up with a group reading of one of the speeches from the play, emphasizing diction and projection, bouncing off consonants, and encouraging the group members to listen to each other so that they can speak the lines together in unison. For variety I will throw in some classic "tongue twisters" too, such as, "The sixth sheik's sixth sheep is sick."

The Folger Shakespeare Library's website (http://www.folger.edu) and their book series *Shakespeare Set Free*, edited by Peggy O'Brien, are two great resources for getting started with a performance-based teaching of Shakespeare in the classroom. The Folger website has numerous helpful resources and activities, many submitted by teachers, for helping a class actively participate in the process of getting to know a Shakespeare play. For more simple theater games, Viola Spolin's *Theatre Games for the Classroom* is very helpful, as is one I use frequently, *Theatre Games for Young Performers*.

HATS AND PROPS

Introducing a few hats and props early in the process is a good way to get the action going. Hats, in particular, provide a nice avenue for giving young actors a non-verbal way of getting into character. In the opening weeks, when students are still holding onto their scripts, a hat can give an actor a way to "feel" like a character. Young actors are natural masters at injecting their own personality into what they wear, and even small choices made with how a hat is worn (jauntily, shadily, cockily, mysteriously) provide a starting point for discussion of specific characters, their traits, and their relationships with other characters. All such discussions always lead back to one thing: the text. "Mining the text" is consistently the best strategy for uncovering the mystery of Shakespeare's language. That is where all the answers lie: in the words themselves.

WHAT DO THE WORDS MEAN?

It is essential that young actors know what they are saying when they recite Shakespeare. If not, they might as well be scat singing, riffing on sounds and rhythm but not conveying a specific meaning. The real question is: What do the words mean? The answer is multifaceted, and can be found in more than one place. The New Folger Library paperback editions of the plays themselves (edited by Barbara Mowat and Paul Werstine, Washington Square Press) are a great resource for understanding Shakespeare's words and passages and "translating" them into modern English. These editions also contain chapters on Shakespeare's language, his life, his theater, a "Modern Perspective," and further reading. There is a wealth of scholarship embedded in these wonderful books, and I make it a point to read them cover to cover before embarking on a play-directing project. At the very least, it is a good idea for any adult who intends to direct a Shakespeare play with a group of students to go through the explanatory notes that appear on the pages facing the text. These explanatory notes are an indispensable "translation tool."

The best way to get students to understand what Shakespeare's words mean is to ask them what they think they mean. Students have their own associations with the words and with how they sound and feel. The best ideas on how to perform Shakespeare often come directly from the students, not from anybody else's notion. If a student has an idea or feeling about a word or passage, and it resonates with her emotionally, physically, or spiritually, then Shakespeare's words can be a vehicle for her feelings. That can result in some powerful performances!

I make it my job as director to read the explanatory notes in the Folger text, but I make it clear to the students that almost "anything goes" when trying to understand Shakespeare. There are no wrong interpretations. Students have their own experiences, with some shared and some uniquely their own. If someone has an association with the phrase "canker-blossom," or if the words make that student or his character feel or act a certain way, then that is the "right" way to decipher it.

I encourage the students to refer to the Folger text's explanatory notes and to keep a pocket dictionary handy. Young actors must attach some meaning to every word or line they recite. If I feel an actor is glossing over a word, I will stop him and ask him what he is saying. If he doesn't know, we will figure it out together as a group.

PROCESS VS. PRODUCT

The process of learning Shakespeare by performing one of his plays is more important than whether everybody remembers his lines or whether somebody misses a cue or an entrance. But my Teaching Artist residencies have always had the end goal of a public performance for about 200 other students, so naturally the performance starts to take precedence over the process somewhere around Dress Rehearsal in the students' minds. It is my job to make sure the actors are prepared—otherwise they will remember the embarrassing moment of a public mistake and not the glorious triumph of owning a Shakespeare play.

In one of my earlier years of play directing, I was sitting in the audience as one of my narrators stood frozen on stage for at least a minute, trying to remember her opening line. I started scrambling in my backpack below my seat for a script, at last prompting her from the audience. Despite her fine performance, that embarrassing moment is all she remembered from the whole experience. Since then I have made sure to assign at least one person to prompt from backstage if necessary. Additionally, I inform the entire cast that if somebody is dying alone out there, it is okay to rescue him or her with an offstage prompt.

There is always a certain amount of stage fright that will accompany a performance, especially a public one for an unfamiliar audience. As a director, I live with stage fright as well, even though I am not appearing on stage. The only antidote to this is work and preparation. If a young actor is struggling with her lines, I make sure to arrange for a session where we run lines over the telephone. I try to set up a buddy system so that students can run lines with their peers, and this often works well. But if somebody does not have a "buddy," I will personally make the time to help out myself. As I assure my students from the outset, I am not going to let them fail or embarrass themselves. They need an experienced leader. And if the leader has experience in teaching but not in directing Shakespeare, then he needs this book!

It is a good idea to culminate in a public performance, as opposed to an in-class project, even if it is only for another classroom. Student actors want to show their newfound Shakespearian thespian skills to an outside group, and this goal motivates them to do a good job. In that respect, "product" is important. Another wonderful bonus to performing a play is that it is a unifying group effort. Students learn teamwork. They learn to give focus to another actor when he is speaking, and to play off of other characters. I like to end each performance with the entire cast reciting a passage in unison. This is a powerful ending, one that reaffirms the unity of the group.

SEEING SHAKESPEARE PERFORMED

It is very helpful for young actors to see Shakespeare performed by a group of professionals, whether they are appearing live on stage (preferable but not always possible) or on film. Because an entire play can take up two or more full class periods, time may be an issue. I am fortunate because thanks to a local foundation that underwrites theater education in the schools, I have been able to take my school groups to a Folger Theatre matinee of the play that they are performing. I always pick a play that is being performed locally that season. But not all group leaders are that lucky. Fortunately, there is the Internet, specifically YouTube. A quick YouTube search for "Shakespeare" can unearth thousands of results, many appropriate for the classroom.

The first "Hamlet" result showed an 18-year-old African-American actor on the streets of Camden, New Jersey, delivering a riveting performance of Hamlet's "The play's the thing." The second clip was from *Cat Head Theatre,* an animation of cats performing Hamlet. Of course, YouTube boasts not just alley cats and feline thespians, but also clips by true legends of the stage, such as John Gielgud and Richard Burton. These clips can be saved and shown in classrooms, providing useful inspiration.

One advantage of the amazing variety of clips available on YouTube is that students can witness the wide range of interpretations for any given scene, speech, or character in Shakespeare, thus freeing them from any preconceived notion that there is a "right" way to do it.

Furthermore, modern interpretations of the Bard may appeal to those who are put off by the "thees and thous" of Elizabethan speech.

By seeing Shakespeare performed either live or on film, students are able to hear the cadence, rhythm, vocal dynamics, and pronunciation of the language, and they can appreciate the life that other actors breathe into the characters. They get to see the story told dramatically, which inspires them to tell their own version.

PUTTING IT ALL TOGETHER: THE STEPS

After a few sessions of theater games to warm up the group, it's time to begin the process of casting the play. Each play cutting in *The 30-Minute Shakespeare* series includes a cast list and a sample program, demonstrating which parts have been divided. Cast size is generally between twenty and thirty students, with major roles frequently assigned to more than one performer. In other words, one student may play Juliet in the first scene, another in the second scene, and yet another in the third. This will distribute the parts evenly so that there is no "star of the show." Furthermore, this prevents actors from being burdened with too many lines. If I have an actor who is particularly talented or enthusiastic, I will give her a bigger role. It is important to go with the grain—one cast member's enthusiasm can be contagious.

I provide the performer of each shared role with a similar headpiece and/or cape, so that the audience can keep track of the characters. When there are sets of twins, I try to use blue shirts and red shirts, so that the audience has at least a fighting chance of figuring it out! Other than these costume consistencies, I rely on the text and the audience's observance to sort out the doubling of characters. Generally, the audience can follow because we are telling the story.

Some participants are shy and do not wish to speak at all on stage. To these students I assign non-speaking parts and technical roles such as sound operator and stage manager. However, I always get everybody on stage at some point, even if it is just for the final group speech, because I want every group member to experience what it is like to be on a stage as part of an ensemble.

CASTING THE PLAY

Young people can be self-conscious and nervous with "formal" auditions, especially if they have little or no acting experience.

I conduct what I call an "informal" audition process. I hand out a questionnaire asking students if there is any particular role that they desire, whether they play a musical instrument. To get a feel for them as people, I also ask them to list one or two hobbies or interests. Occasionally this will inform my casting decisions. If someone can juggle, and the play has the part of a Fool, that skill may come in handy. Dancing or martial arts abilities can also be applied to roles.

For the auditions, I do not use the cut script. I have students stand and read from the Folger edition of the complete text in order to hear how they fare with the longer passages. I encourage them to breathe and carry their vocal energy all the way to the end of a long line of text. I also urge them to play with diction, projection, modulation, and dynamics, elements of speech that we have worked on in our vocal warm-ups and theater games.

I base my casting choices largely on reading ability, vocal strength, and enthusiasm for the project. If someone has requested a particular role, I try to honor that request. I explain that even with a small part, an actor can create a vivid character that adds a lot to the play. Wide variations in personality types can be utilized: if there are two students cast as Romeo, one brooding and one effusive, I try to put the more brooding Romeo in an early lovelorn scene, and place the effusive Romeo in the balcony scene. Occasionally one gets lucky, and the doubling of characters provides a way to match personality types with different aspects of a character's personality. But also be aware of the potential serendipity of non-traditional casting. For example,

I have had one of the smallest students in the class play a powerful Othello. True power comes from within!

Generally, I have more females than males in a class, so women are more likely (and more willing) to play male characters than vice versa. Rare is the high school boy who is brave enough to play a female character, which is unfortunate because it can reap hilarious results.

GET OUTSIDE HELP

Every time there is a fight scene in one of the plays I am directing, I call on my friend Michael Tolaydo, a professional actor and theater professor at St. Mary's College, who is an expert in all aspects of theater, including fight choreography. Not only does Michael stage the fight, but he does so in a way that furthers the action of the play, highlighting character's traits and bringing out the best in the student actors. Fight choreography must be done by an expert or somebody could get hurt. In the absence of such help, super slow-motion fights are always a safe bet and can be quite effective, especially when accompanied by a soundtrack on the boom box.

During dress rehearsals I invite my friend Hilary Kacser. a Washington-area actor and dialect coach for two decades. Because I bring her in late in the rehearsal process, I have her direct her comments to me, which I then filter and relay to the cast. This avoids confusing the cast with a second set of directions. This caveat only applies to general directorial comments from outside visitors. Comments on specific artistic disciplines such as dance, music, and stage combat can come from the outside experts themselves.

If you work in a school, you might have helpful resources within your own building, such as a music or dance teacher who could contribute their expertise to a scene. If nobody is available in your school, try seeking out a member of the local professional theater. Many local performing artists will be glad to help, and the students are usually thrilled to have a visit from a professional performer.

LET STUDENTS BRING THEMSELVES INTO THE PLAY

The best ideas often come from the students themselves. If a young actor has a notion of how to play a scene, I will always give that idea a try. In a rehearsal of *Henry IV, Part 1*, one traveler jumped into the other's arms when they were robbed. It got a huge laugh. This was something that they did on instinct. We kept that bit for the performance, and it worked wonderfully.

As a director, you have to foster an environment in which that kind of spontaneity can occur. The students have to feel safe to experiment. In the same production of *Henry IV*, Falstaff and Hal invented a little fist bump "secret handshake" to use in the battle scene. The students were having fun and bringing parts of themselves into the play. Shakespeare himself would have approved. When possible I try to err on the side of fun because if the young actors are having fun, then they will commit themselves to the project. The beauty of the language, the story, the characters, and the pathos will follow.

There is a balance to be achieved here, however. In that same production of *Henry IV, Part 1*, the student who played Bardolph was having a great time with her character. She carried a leather wineskin around and offered it up to the other characters in the tavern. It was a prop with which she developed a comic relationship. At the end of our thirty-minute *Henry IV, Part 1*, I added a scene from *Henry IV, Part 2* as a coda: The new King Henry V (formerly Falstaff's drinking and carousing buddy Hal) rejects Falstaff, banishing him from within ten miles of the King. It is a sad and sobering moment, one of the most powerful in the play.

But at the performance, in the middle of the King's rejection speech (played by a female student, and her only speech), Bardolph offered her flask to King Henry and got a big laugh, thus not only upstaging the King but also undermining the seriousness and poignancy of the whole scene. She did not know any better; she was bringing herself to the character as I had been encouraging her to do. But it was inappropriate, and in subsequent seasons, if I foresaw something like that happening as an individual joyfully occupied a character, I attempted to prevent it. Some things we cannot predict. Now I make sure to issue a statement warning against changing any of the blocking on show day, and to watch out for upstaging one's peers.

FOUR FORMS OF ENGAGEMENT:
VOCAL, EMOTIONAL, PHYSICAL, AND INTELLECTUAL

When directing a Shakespeare play with a group of students, I always start with the words themselves because the words have the power to engage the emotions, mind, and body. Also, I start with the words in action, as in the previously mentioned exercise, "Positive and Negative Salutations." Students become physically engaged; their bodies react to the images the words evoke. The words have the power to trigger a switch in both the teller and the listener, eliciting both an emotional and physical reaction. I have never heard a student utter the line "Fie! Fie! You counterfeit, you puppet you!" without seeing him change before my eyes. His spine stiffens, his eyes widen, and his fingers point menacingly.

Having used Shakespeare's words to engage the students emotionally and physically, one can then return to the text for a more reflective discussion of what the words mean to us personally. I always make sure to leave at least a few class periods open for discussion of the text, line by line, to ensure that students understand intellectually what they feel viscerally. The advantage to a performance-based teaching of Shakespeare is that by engaging students vocally, emotionally, and physically, it is then much easier to engage them intellectually because they are invested in the words, the characters, and the story. We always start on our feet, and later we sit and talk.

SIX ELEMENTS OF DRAMA: PLOT, CHARACTER, THEME, DICTION, MUSIC, AND SPECTACLE

Over two thousand years ago, Aristotle's *Poetics* outlined six elements of drama, in order of importance: Plot, Character, Theme, Diction, Music, and Spectacle. Because Shakespeare was foremost a playwright, it is helpful to take a brief look at these six elements as they relate to directing a Shakespeare play in the classroom.

PLOT (ACTION)

To Aristotle, plot was the most important element. One of the purposes of *The 30-Minute Shakespeare* is to provide a script that tells Shakespeare's stories, as opposed to concentrating on one scene. In a thirty-minute edit of a Shakespeare play, some plot elements are necessarily omitted. For the sake of a full understanding of the characters' relationships and motivations, it is helpful to make short plot summaries of each scene so that students are aware of their characters' arcs throughout the play. The scene descriptions in the Folger editions are sufficient to fill in the plot holes. Students can read the descriptions aloud during class time to ensure that the story is clear and that no plot elements are neglected. Additionally, there are one-page charts in the Folger editions of *Shakespeare Set Free*, indicating characters' relations graphically, with lines connecting families and factions to give students a visual representation of what can often be complex interrelationships, particularly in Shakespeare's history plays.

Young actors love action. That is why *The 30-Minute Shakespeare* includes dynamic blocking (stage direction) that allows students to tell the story in a physically dramatic fashion. Characters' movements on the stage are always motivated by the text itself.

CHARACTER

I consider myself a facilitator and a director more than an acting teacher. I want the students' understanding of their characters to spring from the text and the story. From there, I encourage them to consider how their character might talk, walk, stand, sit, eat, and drink. I also urge students to consider characters' motivations, objectives, and relationships, and I will ask pointed questions to that end during the rehearsal process. I try not to show the students how I would perform a scene, but if no ideas are forthcoming from anybody in the class, I will suggest a minimum of two possibilities for how the character might respond.

At times students may want more guidance and examples. Over thirteen years of directing plays in the classroom, I have wavered between wanting all the ideas to come from the students, and deciding that I need to be more of a "director," telling them what I would like to see them doing. It is a fine line, but in recent years I have decided that if I don't see enough dynamic action or characterization, I will step in and "direct" more. But I always make sure to leave room for students to bring themselves into the characters because their own ideas are invariably the best.

THEME (THOUGHTS, IDEAS)

In a typical English classroom, theme will be a big topic for discussion of a Shakespeare play. Using a performance-based method of teaching Shakespeare, an understanding of the play's themes develops from "mining the text" and exploring Shakespeare's words and his story. If the students understand what they are saying and how that relates to their characters and the overall story, the plays' themes will emerge clearly. We always return to the text itself. There are a number of elegant computer programs, such as www.wordle.net, that will count the number of recurring words in a passage and illustrate them graphically. For example, if the word "jealousy" comes up more than any other word in *Othello,* it will appear in a larger font. Seeing the words displayed by size in this way can offer up illuminating insights into the interaction between words in the text and the play's themes. Your computer-minded students might enjoy searching for such tidbits. There are more internet tools and websites in the Additional Resources section at the back of this book.

I cannot overstress the importance of acting out the play in understanding its themes. By embodying the roles of Othello and Iago and reciting their words, students do not simply comprehend the themes intellectually, but understand them kinesthetically, physically, and emotionally. They are essentially **living** the characters' jealousy, pride, and feelings about race. The themes of appearance vs. reality, good vs. evil, honesty, misrepresentation, and self-knowledge (or lack thereof) become physically felt as well as intellectually understood. Performing Shakespeare delivers a richer understanding than that which comes from just reading the play. Students can now relate the characters' conflicts to their own struggles.

DICTION (LANGUAGE)

If I had to cite one thing I would like my actors to take from their experience of performing a play by William Shakespeare, it is an appreciation and understanding of the beauty of Shakespeare's language. The language is where it all begins and ends. Shakespeare's stories are dramatic, his characters are rich and complex, and his settings are exotic and fascinating, but it is through his language that these all achieve their richness. This leads me to spend more time on language than on any other element of the performance.

Starting with daily vocal warm-ups, many of them using parts of the script or other Shakespearean passages, I consistently emphasize the importance of the words. Young actors often lack experience in speaking clearly and projecting their voices outward, so in addition to comprehension, I emphasize projection, diction, breathing, pacing, dynamics, coloring of words, and vocal energy. *Theatre Games for Young Performers* contains many effective vocal exercises, as does the Folger's *Shakespeare Set Free* series. Consistent emphasis on all aspects of Shakespeare's language, especially on how to speak it effectively, is the most important element to any Shakespeare performance with a young cast.

MUSIC

A little music can go a long way in setting a mood for a thirty-minute Shakespeare play. I usually open the show with a short passage of music to set the tone. Thirty seconds of music played on a boom box operated by a student can provide a nice introduction to the play, create an atmosphere for the audience, and give the actors a sense of place and feeling.

iTunes is a good starting point for choosing your music. Typing in "Shakespeare" or "Hamlet" or "jealousy" (if you are going for a theme) will result in an excellent selection of aural performance enhancers at the very reasonable price of ninety-nine cents each (or free of charge, see Additional Resources section.) Likewise, fight sounds, foreboding sounds, weather sounds (rain, thunder), trumpet sounds, etc. are all readily available online at affordable cost. I typically include three sound cues in a play, just enough to enhance but not overpower a production. The boom box operator sits on the far right or left of the stage, not backstage, so he can see the action. This also has the added benefit of having somebody out there with a script, capable of prompting in a pinch.

SPECTACLE

Aristotle considered spectacle the least important aspect of drama. Students tend to be surprised at this since we are used to being bombarded with production values on TV and video, often at the expense of substance. In my early days of putting on student productions, I would find myself hamstrung by my own ambitions in the realm of scenic design.

A simple bench or two chairs set on the stage are sufficient. The sense of "place" can be achieved through language and acting. Simple set dressing, a few key props, and some tasteful, emblematic costume pieces will go a long way toward providing all the "spectacle" you need.

In the stage directions to the plays in *The 30-Minute Shakespeare* series, I make frequent use of two large pillars stage left and right at the Folger Shakespeare Library's Elizabethan Theatre. I also have characters frequently entering and exiting from "stage rear." Your stage will have a different layout. Take a good look at the performing space you will be using and see if there are any elements that can be incorporated into your own stage directions. Is there a balcony? Can characters enter from the audience? (Make sure that they can get there from backstage, unless you want them waiting in the lobby until their entrance, which may be impractical.) If possible, make sure to rehearse in that space a few times to fix any technical issues and perhaps discover a few fun staging variations that will add pizzazz and dynamics to your own show.

The real spectacle is in the telling of the tale. Wooden swords are handy for characters that need them. Students should be warned at the outset that playing with swords outside of the scene is verboten. Letters, moneybags, and handkerchiefs should all have plentiful duplicates kept in a small prop box, as well as with a stage manager, because they tend to disappear in the hands of adolescents. After every rehearsal and performance, I recommend you personally sweep the rehearsal or performance area immediately for stray props. It is amazing what gets left behind.

Ultimately, the performances are about language and human drama, not set pieces, props, and special effects. Fake blood, glitter, glass, and liquids have no place on the stage; they are a recipe for disaster, or, at the very least, a big mess. On the other hand, the props that are employed can often be used effectively to convey character, as in Bardolph's aforementioned relationship with his wineskin.

PITFALLS AND SOLUTIONS

Putting on a play in a high school classroom is not easy. There are problems with enthusiasm, attitude, attention, and line memorization, to name a few. As anybody who has directed a play will tell you, it is always darkest before the dawn. My experience is that after one or two days of utter despair just before the play goes up, show day breaks and the play miraculously shines. To quote a recurring gag in one of my favorite movies, *Shakespeare in Love:* "It's a mystery."

ENTHUSIASM, FRUSTRATION, AND DISCIPLINE

Bring the enthusiasm yourself. Feed on the energy of the eager students, and others will pick up on that. Keep focused on the task at hand. Arrive prepared. Enthusiasm comes as you make headway. Ultimately, it helps to remind the students that a "play" is fun. I try to focus on the positive attributes of the students, rather than the ones that drive me crazy. This is easier said than done, but it is important. One season, I yelled at the group two days in a row. On day two of yelling, they tuned me out, and it took me a while to win them back. I learned my lesson; since then I've tried not to raise my voice out of anger or frustration. As I grow older and more mature, it is important for me to lead by example. It has been years since I yelled at a student group. If I am disappointed in their work or their behavior, I will express my disenchantment in words, speaking from the heart as somebody who cares about them and cares about our performance and our experience together. I find that fundamentally, young people want to please, to do well, and to be liked. If there is a serious discipline problem, I will hand it over to the regular classroom teacher, the administrator, or the parent.

LINE MEMORIZATION

Students may have a hard time memorizing lines. In these cases, see if you can pair them up with a "buddy" and existing friend who will run lines with them in person or over the phone after school. If students do not have such a "buddy," I volunteer to run lines with them myself. If serious line memorization problems arise that cannot be solved through work, then two students can switch parts if it is early enough in the rehearsal process. For doubled roles, the scene with fewer lines can go to the actor who is having memorization problems. Additionally, a few passages or lines can be cut. Again, it is important to address these issues early. Later cuts become more problematic as other actors have already memorized their cues. I have had to do late cuts about twice in thirteen years. While they have gotten us out of jams, it is best to assess early whether a student will have line memorization problems, and deal with the problem sooner rather than later.

In production, always keep several copies of the script backstage, as well as cheat sheets indicating cues, entrances, and scene changes. Make a prop list, indicating props for each scene, as well as props that are the responsibility of individual actors. Direct the Stage Manager and an Assistant Stage Manager to keep track of these items, and on show days, personally double-check if you can.

In thirteen years of preparing an inner-city public high school English class for a public performance on a field trip to the Folger Secondary School Shakespeare Festival, my groups and I have been beset by illness, emotional turmoil, discipline problems, stage fright, adolescent angst, midlife crises (not theirs), and all manner of other emergencies, including acts of God and nature. Despite the difficulties and challenges inherent in putting on a Shakespeare play with a group of young people, one amazing fact stands out in my experience. Here is how many times a student has been absent for show day: Zero. Somehow, everybody has always made it to the show, and the show has gone on. How can this be? It's a mystery.

✳ PERFORMANCE NOTES:
THE TWO GENTLEMEN OF VERONA

I directed this performance of *The Two Gentlemen of Verona* in 2001 with a Washington, D.C. public school ninth grade English class. These notes are the result of my own review of the performance video. They are not intended to be the "definitive" performance notes for all productions of *The Two Gentlemen of Verona*. Your production will be unique to you and your cast. That is the magic of live theater. What is interesting about these notes is that many of the performance details I mention were not part of the original stage directions. They either emerged spontaneously on performance day or were developed by students in rehearsal after the stage directions had been written into the script. Some of these pieces of stage business might work like a charm. Others may fall flat. My favorites are the ones that arise directly from the students themselves, and demonstrate a union between actor and character, as if that individual has become a vehicle for the character he is playing. To witness a fourteen-year-old young man "become" Valentine as Shakespeare's words leave his mouth is a memorable moment indeed.

SCENE 1 (ACT I, SCENE II)

Courtly music at the top of the play sets the mood for the audience. Lucetta is dusting the furniture. Simple physical motions give us a sense of place and also indicate the occupation and status of the character. This first scene between Julia and her waiting woman Lucetta provides some entertaining nuances regarding status: after Lucetta says, "I do not like this tune," Julia gives her a little pinch.

Lucetta responds by pinching Julia, Julia then slaps Lucetta on the arm, and Lucetta immediately slaps her back. This combative little interchange gets a laugh from the audience. It also serves to illustrate that although Julia is Lucetta's boss, they are on equal footing in many respects. Lucetta is also Julia's friend and confidante, and she is comfortable enough in her relationship to fight with her playfully. Nonetheless, on Julia's line, "Get you gone, and let the papers lie," it remains clear that Julia is the boss.

This status disparity is reinforced in the interchange that follows Julia's reading of the ripped pieces of the letter. Lucetta chides Julia for leaving the papers on the floor, and Julia recommends that Lucetta pick them up. Lucetta here begins her speech by refusing: "Nay I was taken up for laying them down." After a pause, she acquiesces, but not before trying to make it sound as if it were her own idea: "Yet here they shall not lie, for catching cold."

The letter should be torn into several pieces, not just two. The humor arises from Julia's attempts to put the small pieces of the letter together and from her difficulty reading the tiny segments. When she kisses each individual section of paper, one could become stuck on her tongue, causing her to talk funny. She could accidentally swallow one of the papers, and Lucetta could save her from choking with a Heimlich maneuver. Encourage students to exaggerate—and then ask them if they can exaggerate even more.

Often by going "over the top," we surprise the audience into laughter. This first scene contains broad physical comedy, and it benefits from expansive, exaggerated movements from the actors. The farther they take the physical comedy, by committing to big movements and silliness, the more fun they have with it, and the audience picks up on the merriment.

How do we "take it farther"? One simple exercise is to play a theatrical moment four different ways: small, normal, bigger, and over-the-top. "Small" entails purposefully saying one's line in an almost inaudible whisper with little body movement. Most participants agree that there is not much sense in delivering a line that the audience can't hear.

"Normal" means "as if one were sitting in a room talking." The actor makes no additional effort to project or enunciate, nor does she try to emote. When an actor recites a line of Shakespeare in "normal" mode, other players usually find this lacking too. Sometimes I point out to them that this is actually what I am seeing and hearing when they think they are performing at "bigger," the next level.

"Bigger" implies a level of exaggeration or stylization that is a hallmark of stage acting: chewing the words, holding a gesture or pose slightly larger and longer than usual, and projecting as if one were trying to reach the back row. It also calls for a greater vocal range: the words take on a more sing-song quality, the pitch gets higher and lower, and the facial expressions are more pronounced. If you are lucky, your actors will achieve this third level in their performance.

The final level, "over-the-top," is the most useful in comedy, but also helpful with beginning actors in any genre. In "over-the-top," I encourage my thespians to throw caution to the wind and see just how big, loud, exaggerated, and ridiculous they can be, without regard to whether it makes sense for the scene. I am essentially asking them to go beyond their perceived limits of decorum. I assure them that it is impossible for them to overact or over-exaggerate in this exercise. I am asking for systematic and purposeful breaking of boundaries. This is where it gets interesting, because frequently what young actors give me at this stage is exactly what I want! Nobody ever goes too far, and what many young actors consider "over-the-top" is actually what I see as the proper level of exaggeration for a silly comedy. The most important lesson to be derived from this exercise is that there is a great range of possibilities and we often don't know what the scope is until we experiment with stretching our limits. This exercise can be applied to just vocals, as well as speech combined with movement.

SCENE 2 (ACT II, SCENE III)

The narrator explains that in this scene, Launce chastises his dog, Crab, for not sharing his grief about parting with his family. She then walks offstage holding the back of her hand to her brow in a "woe is me" gesture, setting a lighthearted tone for the upcoming clown monologue.

The young man playing the dog does an admirable job of conveying the clueless loyalty of Crab. He wears a cap with floppy ears and plunks himself by Launce's side for the duration of the speech, staring blankly toward the audience with a faint smile on his face. When Launce removes his shoes for use in the puppet show explanation of his parentage, Crab quickly moves away, as if the shoes have an unpleasant odor to them, a moment the audience enjoys.

We chose to have an actor play the part of Crab, though we could have used a stuffed animal in his place. Generally, a live actor is preferable. The most important element to playing an animal is not to overact, and the actor playing Crab had the proper sense of stillness that made the portrayal complete. Although many comic bits hinge on physical exaggeration, in others, such as with this scene, less is more.

There are numerous comic possibilities in Launce's "shoe puppetry." He kisses his shoes as if he were kissing his parents. One shoe has a hole in it. One shoe weeps. One shoe smells like his mother's breath. Launce could put a bonnet on one shoe and a hat on the other to represent his mother and father. When he gets confused as to whether or not he plays the part of the dog, Launce might put his hat on the dog and put the dog's collar on himself. With the shoes on his hands, he could act out a little two-step in the air. Crab can cock his head while curiously attempting to follow Launce's reasoning— and after Launce complains that Crab "speaks not a word," he can look over at Crab, who exclaims, "Woof!" To exploit this silly scene for all its potential laughs, experiment with the comic possibilities in rehearsal and encourage your class to free-associate and chime in.

SCENE 3 (ACT II, SCENE IV)

The narrator enters to describe the scene, accompanied by Crab the Dog on a leash. At the end of her narration, she looks at Crab as if awaiting a translation. Crab says, "Woof." Running gags are a good comedic trick. Ideally, I would have repeated this "woof" a third time; when possible, employ the rule of three in comedy.

When Valentine stands to greet Proteus, the two exchange an embrace that suggests a close friendship. When Proteus first lays eyes on Silvia, even before he sits down, there is a pause in which he stops in his tracks and just looks at her. In this way the audience receives foreshadowing of Proteus's attraction to Silvia. Valentine too can notice this attraction. When Silvia exits, Valentine occupies the chair where she was sitting and asks Proteus, "How does your lady?" The emphasis is on the word "your," as if Valentine is trying to draw the conversation away from Silvia. These are subtle acting points, but when played with the proper timing and attention to detail, they provide the audience with the subtext necessary to appreciate the nascent conflict between two friends who both admire the same woman.

Both Valentine's and Proteus's speeches in the latter part of the scene contain rich language that must be colored by the actors to achieve their full poetical resonance. The following is a selection of Valentine's words from just four lines of text: "world," "rich," "jewel," "twenty," "seas," "sand," "pearl," "water," "nectar," "rocks," and "gold." And here are some of Proteus's words from his final, amorous speech in the scene: "heat," "nail," "strength," "drives," "remembrance," "former," "love," "newer," "object," "eye," "praise," "true," "perfection," "reasonless," "waxen," "fire," "impression," "erring," "love," "compass," and "skill." Each of these words alone is expressive, and when spoken as part of a line of Shakespeare, they are poetical.

How does one speak "poetically"? The first rule is not to rush the phrases. Many young actors hurry their lines, which perplexes the audience. Writing down beats and breathing points in the script helps curb this problem. Have the actors mark a slash in their text at appropriate breathing points. They can also underline words or syllables that are accentuated, and then experiment with changing the emphasis to hear how this changes a line's meaning.

Actors can practice "coloring" their words. Think of the word as not just a word, but also an emotion evoker. See if the word can become a poem in itself, with a richness that echoes its sentiment or enhances the image it arouses. Marking beats and coloring words will encourage actors to slow down their speech. Proteus's closing speech, when expressed colorfully, not only advances the plot and conflict, but it also gives the audience a good taste of some of Shakespeare's rich and poetic language.

SCENE 4 (ACT III, SCENE I)

Valentine tries to deliver the elopement love letter to Silvia and is stopped by the Duke. Although this is not a comic scene per se (inasmuch as it results in Valentine's anguish over her banishment), the actors still get some laughs from the setup. Valentine walks from stage right to left, pretending not to see the Duke. His gait is casual, yet swift. When the Duke calls out, "Whither away so fast?" Valentine freezes and slowly turns his head out toward the audience with a forced grin on his face. Valentine delivers his excuse to the Duke and continues to walk swiftly offstage, but the Duke reaches his arm out fully and grabs onto the back of Valentine's collar. Valentine's feet keep moving, but since the Duke is holding him back, he goes nowhere, which gets a laugh.

When the Duke reads the contents, the mood shifts suddenly to anger. He delivers the banishment speech furiously, finishing by throwing the letter to the ground and exiting. Here we see a powerful man protecting his family. The Duke can use his sword to punctuate his speech, pointing it upward on the line, "By heaven," and pointing it at Valentine's throat on "as thou lovest life."

The mood shifts yet a third time as Valentine falls to his knees following the Duke's exit and exclaims, "And why not death, rather than living torment?" Thus, in three short but poetically powerful interchanges within one scene, the audience has experienced laughter, anger, and sorrow. When acted dynamically, this scene not only tells a story, but also takes us on an emotional journey.

Launce's entrance brings us back to laughter as he threatens an imaginary foe with his sword and mistakes the word "vanished" for "banished." I love how quickly the moods change in this scene, which ends with mixed emotions. Proteus comforts a grieving Valentine, but the audience now knows that it is false comfort and part of a greater plot by Proteus to thwart his friend and steal his woman. If the players are sufficiently aware of the subtleties and subtext in this scene, by fully understanding the plot and relationships through pre-show study and discussion of the text, they will better be able to tell the complicated tale.

Launce sums up the paradox aptly with this line:

"I am but a fool, look you; and yet I have the wit to think
My master is a kind of knave."

SCENE 5 (ACT IV, SCENE II)

Musicians serenade Silvia on Proteus's behalf, while Julia, disguised as a male page, looks on. Always on the lookout for funny moments, we decided that one of our singers was going to be a little "off," and repeat the final line of each verse after the rest of the musicians, thus discombobulating them. This works well during the performance, and at the end of the musical interlude the rest of the musicians chase the "off" musician offstage, yelling at him at the top of their lungs, to great audience laughter.

Since the set lacks a balcony, Silvia stands on a bench while Proteus woos her, as though looking down at him from a much greater height. Julia is concealed behind the stage right pillar, but occasionally we see her face peer out woefully as she reacts to Proteus's amorous overtures. After Proteus's line, "and to your shadow I will make true love," Julia, still behind the pillar, says to the Host, "If 'twere a substance, you would, sure, deceive it." One possibility for your production is to have Silvia and Proteus freeze in place on this line, as if time is standing still for Julia's aside to the host. This also gives the focus to Julia as she speaks.

When a character in the play disguises herself for a scene, it can throw the audience off, since they may be unfamiliar with the story. In these cases, having a narrator explain this plot point prior to the scene is especially helpful. The actor playing Julia must also work hard to convey her heartbreak with her facial expressions, body language, and vocal tone.

SCENE 6 (ACT V, SCENE IV)

Our final scene begins with a musical intro, to set a mysterious tone for the new forest setting. The sound cue is called "mysterious forest music." If you have a student interested in sound effects, have him research them online. There are also some free sound effects resources listed in the appendix of this book. In the absence of elaborate lights and sets, a small musical cue can go a long way toward setting a mood or tone.

This is a menacing and disturbing scene, as it culminates in Proteus's attempt to force himself on Silvia. Shakespeare is not one to shy away from ugly situations. In this production, we decided to give Silvia the upper hand. As Proteus lunges at her, she eludes and then attacks him. Proteus ends up on the ground with Silvia stepping on him. This has the twofold effect of inserting humor into a scene that was veering rather close to tragedy. By overpowering Proteus, Silvia brings the audience back into laughter, which is where we want them to be at the end of a comedy. When Silvia says, "O heaven," it is not said in fear, but with tongue-in-cheek self-satisfaction—and the audience responds with gleeful cheering.

Julia comes out of hiding, still dressed as a boy, and performs an elaborate multi-part fainting move that sets us firmly back into the land of comedy. After Julia reveals her true identity to Proteus, he begins his final redemption speech facing out toward the audience. Then, on his final line, he turns to face his original beloved, Julia:

"What is in Silvia's face, but I may spy
More fresh in Julia's with a constant eye?"

The play resolves with the promise of two marriages, and all ends well in our Shakespeare comedy. The musicians and cast stand together on the stage, swaying back and forth together in rhythm, clapping and chanting, "One peace, one house, one mutual happiness!"

The students began the process of rehearsing *The Two Gentlemen of Verona* as D.C. public school ninth graders, but by play's end they were Shakespearean actors. May this be your story too. Using this book as a guideline, I hope that the experience of performing the play will bring delight and laughter to both actors and audiences alike.

✳ *THE TWO GENTLEMEN OF VERONA:* SET AND PROP LIST

SET PIECES:

> Table
> Two chairs
> Bench
> Throne

PROPS:

THROUGHOUT:

> Swords

SCENE 1:

> Letter for Lucetta
> Flowers for table
> Tea pot and cups for table

SCENE 2:

> Long leash for Crab the dog
> Oversized shoes for Launce, one with a hole

SCENE 4:

> Letter for Valentine

SCENE 5:

> Tambourines or musical instruments for Musicians

SCENE 6:

> Two rings for Julia

BENJAMIN BANNEKER ACADEMIC HIGH SCHOOL *presents*

Two Gentlemen of Verona
By William Shakespeare

9th Grade English Class | Instructor: Cleve Bryant | Guest Director: Nick Newlin

CAST OF CHARACTERS:

Scene 1:
Narrator: Kirby York
Julia, in love with Proteus: Kara Hughley
Lucetta, Julia's waiting woman: Brittany Hill

Scene 2:
Narrator: LaShawn Parker
Launce, servant to Proteus: Jeremy Williams
Speed, Servant to Valentine: David Lesley
Crab, Launce's Dog: Christopher Brown

Scene 3:
Narrator: Christopher Brown, with Jeremy Williams
Silvia, daughter of the Duke of Milan, in love with Valentine: LaShawn Parker
Valentine, a young lover and gentleman: Michael Glenn
Proteus, unfaithful friend to Valentine: Jeff Balough

Scene 4:
Narrator: Chinyere Offor
Duke of Milan: Randy Harper
Proteus: Jeff Balough
Valentine: Brandon Jones
Launce: Jeremy Williams

Scene 5:
Narrator: Falone Amoa
Proteus: Jeff Balough
Host: Brittani Kirkendoll
Julia (as Sebastian): Rhonesha Buford
Silvia: Lauren Blassingame
Musicians: Leroy Gray, Aba Tyus, Jeremy Williams, Christopher Brown

Scene 6:
Narrator: Aba Tyus
Valentine: Michael Glenn
Proteus: Jeff Balough
Silvia: Chinyere Offor
Julia: Falone Amoa
Duke of Milan: Kirby York

Stage Crew:
Sets, props: Dexter Mackie, Constantine Olumba, Leroy Gray
Sets, costumes: Jinat Tabasum, Aba Tyus, Falone Amoa, Kirby York
Stage Manager: Leroy Gray

"In love, who respects friend?"

ADDITIONAL RESOURCES

SHAKESPEARE

*Shakespeare Set Free: Teaching Romeo
and Juliet, Macbeth and a Midsummer
Night's Dream*
Peggy O'Brien, Ed., Teaching
Shakespeare Institute
Washington Square Press
New York, 1993

*Shakespeare Set Free: Teaching Hamlet
and Henry IV, Part 1*
Peggy O'Brien, Ed., Teaching
Shakespeare Institute
Washington Square Press
New York, 1994

*Shakespeare Set Free: Teaching Twelfth
Night and Othello*
Peggy O'Brien, Ed., Teaching
Shakespeare Institute
Washington Square Press
New York, 1995

The *Shakespeare Set Free* series is
an invaluable resource with lesson
plans, activites, handouts, and
excellent suggestions for rehearsing
and performing Shakespeare plays in a
classroom setting.

ShakesFear and How to Cure It!
Ralph Alan Cohen
Prestwick House, Inc.
Delaware, 2006

*The Friendly Shakespeare:
A Thoroughly Painless Guide
to the Best of the Bard*
Norrie Epstein
Penguin Books
New York, 1994

Brush Up Your Shakespeare!
Michael Macrone
Cader Books
New York, 1990

*Shakespeare's Insults:
Educating Your Wit*
Wayne F. Hill and Cynthia J. Ottchen
Three Rivers Press
New York, 1991

*Practical Approaches to
Teaching Shakespeare*
Peter Reynolds
Oxford University Press
New York, 1991

Scenes From Shakespeare:
A Workbook for Actors
Robin J. Holt
McFarland and Co.
London, 1988

THEATER AND PERFORMANCE

Impro: Improvisation and the Theatre
Keith Johnstone
Routledge Books
London, 1982

A Dictionary of Theatre Anthropology:
The Secret Art of the Performer
Eugenio Barba and Nicola Savarese
Routledge
London, 1991

THEATER GAMES

Theatre Games for Young Performers
Maria C. Novelly
Meriwether Publishing
Colorado, 1990

Improvisation for the Theater
Viola Spolin
Northwestern University Press
Illinois, 1983

Theater Games for Rehearsal:
A Director's Handbook
Viola Spolin
Northwestern University Press
Illinois, 1985

101 Theatre Games for Drama
Teachers, Classroom Teachers
& Directors
Mila Johansen
Players Press Inc.
California, 1994

PLAY DIRECTING

Theater and the Adolescent Actor:
Building a Successful School Program
Camille L. Poisson
Archon Books
Connecticut, 1994

Directing for the Theatre
W. David Sievers
Wm. C. Brown, Co.
Iowa, 1965

The Director's Vision: Play Direction
from Analysis to Production
Louis E. Catron
Mayfield Publishing Co.
California, 1989

INTERNET RESOURCES

http://www.folger.edu
The Folger Shakespeare Library's
website has lesson plans, primary
sources, study guides, images,
workshops, programs for teachers
and students, and much more. The
definitive Shakespeare website for
educators, historians and all lovers
of the Bard.

http://www.shakespeare.mit.edu.
The Complete Works of
William Shakespeare.
All complete scripts for *The
30-Minute Shakespeare* series were
originally downloaded from this site
before editing. Links to other internet
resources.

http://www.LoMonico.com/
Shakespeare-and-Media.htm
http://shakespeare-and-media
.wikispaces.com
Michael LoMonico is Senior
Consultant on National Education
for the Folger Shakespeare Library.
His *Seminar Shakespeare 2.0* offers a
wealth of information on how to use
exciting new approaches and online
resources for teaching Shakespeare.

http://www.freesound.org.
A collaborative database of sounds
and sound effects.

http://www.wordle.net.
A program for creating "word clouds"
from the text that you provide. The
clouds give greater prominence to
words that appear more frequently in
the source text.

http://www.opensourceshakespeare
.org.
This site has good searching capacity.

http://shakespeare.palomar.edu/
default.htm
Excellent links and searches

http://shakespeare.com/
Write like Shakespeare,
Poetry Machine, tag cloud

http://www.shakespeare-online.com/

http://www.bardweb.net/

http://www.rhymezone.com/
shakespeare/
Good searchable word and phrase
finder.
Or by lines:
http://www.rhymezone.com/
shakespeare/toplines/

http://shakespeare.mcgill.ca/
Shakespeare and Performance
research team

http://www.enotes.com/william-
shakespeare

Needless to say, the internet goes on and on with valuable Shakespeare resources.
The ones listed here are excellent starting points and will set you on your way in the
great adventure that is Shakespeare.

NICK NEWLIN has been performing the comedy and variety act *Nicolo Whimsey* for international audiences for 25 years. Since 1996, he has conducted an annual play directing residency affiliated with the Folger Shakespeare Library in Washington, D.C. Newlin received a BA with Honors from Harvard University in 1982 and an MA in Theater with an emphasis in Play Directing from the University of Maryland in 1996.

THE 30-MINUTE SHAKESPEARE

AS YOU LIKE IT
978-1-935550-06-8

**THE COMEDY
OF ERRORS**
978-1-935550-08-2

HAMLET
978-1-935550-24-2

HENRY IV, PART 1
978-1-935550-11-2

HENRY V
978-1-935550-38-9

JULIUS CAESAR
978-1-935550-29-7

KING LEAR
978-1-935550-09-9

**LOVE'S LABOR'S
LOST**
978-1-935550-07-5

MACBETH
978-1-935550-02-0

**A MIDSUMMER
NIGHT'S DREAM**
978-1-935550-00-6

**THE MERCHANT
OF VENICE**
978-1-935550-32-7

**THE MERRY WIVES
OF WINDSOR**
978-1-935550-05-1

**MUCH ADO ABOUT
NOTHING**
978-1-935550-03-7

OTHELLO
978-1-935550-10-5

RICHARD III
978-1-935550-39-6

ROMEO AND JULIET
978-1-935550-01-3

**THE TAMING OF THE
SHREW**
978-1-935550-33-4

THE TEMPEST
978-1-935550-28-0

TWELFTH NIGHT
978-1-935550-04-4

**THE TWO
GENTLEMEN OF
VERONA**
978-1-935550-25-9

**THE 30-MINUTE SHAKESPEARE
ANTHOLOGY**
978-1-935550-33-4

All plays $9.95, available in print and eBook editions in bookstores everywhere

*"A truly fun, emotional, and sometimes magical first experience . . . guided by
a sagacious, knowledgeable, and intuitive educator."* —Library Journal

PHOTOCOPYING AND PERFORMANCE RIGHTS

There is no royalty for performing any series of *The 30-Minute Shakespeare* in
a classroom or on a stage. The publisher hereby grants unlimited photocopy
permission for one series of performances to all acting groups that have
purchased the play. If a group stages a performance, please post a comment
and/or photo to our Facebook page; we'd love to hear about it!

CPSIA information can be obtained
at www.ICGtesting.com
Printed in the USA
JSHW051401180723
44982JS00009B/335